Exploring Personality Styles

Exploring Personality Styles

A Guide for Better Understanding Yourself and Your Colleagues

Michael Dobson

SkillPath Publications
Mission, KS

Project Editor: Kelly Scanlon

Editor: Jane Doyle Guthrie

Page Layout: Premila Malik Borchardt

Cover Design: Rod Hankins

ISBN: 1-57294-124-3

Library of Congress Catalog Card Number: 97-068592

22   07 08 09 10 11

Printed in the United States of America

For the improper Bostonians

Edward Smith (INFP)

Lane Lambert (ENFJ)

Margie Thornton (ENFP)

and for

Rod Jurado

trainer and colleague

for research support and advice

Contents

Introduction

As Butch Cassidy once said to the Sundance Kid, "Who are those guys, anyway?"

Sometimes we find ourselves asking this question about our colleagues, our staff members, our bosses, and our customers. We live and work every day with a wide assortment of people, each with his or her own agenda, goals, and above all, styles. We know that we should—and must—value diversity in the workplace, because the differences among team members can add to productivity, expand creative options, and make our organization more effective. But variety also has its downside—it can be more difficult to work with people when we don't know who they are or where they're coming from.

Much of the conflict and tension we may experience in the office isn't necessarily about which of our co-workers suffers from the famous psychological condition "OPD" (Obnoxious

Personality Disorder)—although we frequently act as if this is the case. Instead, the problem often comes down to natural differences in style and temperament: the characteristics that make us distinct individuals who value and prefer different behaviors, different job assignments, different communication approaches, and different goals.

Style differences are distinct from the concepts of "difficult people" and "cultural diversity."

The difference between "difficult" and "different" may sometimes seem narrow indeed. When someone acts in a way that conflicts with us, we tend to label that person "difficult." However, difficult behavior is distinguished by its planned nature. People who throw temper tantrums to get their own way have actually made a choice, based on evidence, to behave in that way because it works for them. On the other hand, people who are much faster or slower in their daily pace than you—however "difficult" it may be for you to cope with that behavior—are exhibiting a "difference."

Cultural diversity is the recognition that one's cultural background and heritage can also influence one's behavior. Different styles of bargaining, different choices about how much personal body space is needed, even different senses of the meaning of time have been attributed to cultural patterns. Even within cultural patterns, however, people still can be "difficult people" or not; they can exhibit different personality styles.

This book isn't about difficult people or cultural diversity. Instead, it explores the concept of "personality styles": the idea that people have fundamental differences in outlook, behavior, and style. You can identify certain style characteristics and use those characteristics to improve your understanding of other people, to work more effectively with them, to solve problems and resolve conflicts with them, and to achieve your goals.

To get the fullest value from an understanding of personality styles, you first must understand your own. Like everyone else, you have preferences, approaches, and communication issues. If you find someone else difficult to relate to, chances are that person feels the same way about you. If you learn to relate to that person more effectively, he or she will automatically relate better to you.

The most important thing to realize about personality styles is they are not about right or wrong, good or bad—they're about differences. How to understand them. How to appreciate them. How to work with them effectively.

Further, when you have a grasp of other people's values, needs, and approaches to work and life, you can adjust your own style and approach to be more effective. That's the primary value of using style approaches to personality. While it's obvious that in-depth personal knowledge beats general knowledge, general knowledge about someone's personality type is dramatically better than no knowledge at all!

By reading this handbook and using the suggestions and exercises in it, you will gain the following:

- An understanding of the basic history and foundation of personality style measurement systems

- An overview of the various instruments you may encounter in your own organization

- A determination of your own style as well as those of others around you

Exploring Personality Styles contains a basic model you can use for yourself and your team members, easy both to use and to apply. You can gain useful insights about the people around you even if you can't get them to take a test. If you find this model useful, you may wish to expand your study of temperament and related issues. A suggested reading list appears at the back for that purpose.

Personality Style Indicators

Nearly twenty-five centuries ago, Hippocrates identified four "temperaments" or personality types: choleric (hot-tempered), phlegmatic (calm), melancholic (depressed), and sanguine (cheerful). He believed that the body's organs produced an excess of bile, phlegm, black bile, and blood (the four "humors"), and whichever substance was produced in excess determined a person's basic personality type. While the association between body fluids and temperament isn't supported by medical evidence, the idea of different personality styles, or temperaments, has come in and out of fashion among psychologists. Today, the idea that basic personality types exist and differ among people is well-accepted.

A number of psychologists studied temperaments and personality types in the early years of the twentieth century, all beginning from their own perspective but ending with types comparable to Hippocrates's paradigm. However, the temperament model eventually fell out of popularity.

In the 1950s, Isabel Myers studied Carl Jung's work on psychological types, and with her mother Katheryn Briggs developed the Myers-Briggs Type Indicator (MBTI), which led to a revival of the concept. The MBTI is today widely used in business and education. Not by accident, the sixteen Myers-Briggs personality types can also be grouped into four temperaments.

A number of different models are popular in today's workplace. Although similar in some respects, each is designed to achieve certain goals. You may encounter the Personal Profile System (PPS), more commonly known as the DiSC model, the Wilson, Tracom System, or the Alessandra "Platinum Rule" model. There are many others as well.

As you learn about these different models, you'll find that some are described as "tested and validated," while others are not. The process of field-testing and validation involves a formal study with a statistically representative sample of subjects to determine whether the characteristics identified by the model verifiably exist in the people being tested. The MBTI and PPS are tested and validated instruments. Many other popular tools, including the *Personality Explorer™* used later in this book, have not undergone such research or analysis, although they've probably been administered to thousands of people nationwide. The key to using personality style models (whether validated or not) is to understand what they can do well—and what they can't.

How to Use a Style Indicator

Can you really take all the people in the world, put them into four little boxes called "styles," and claim you now understand them? Of course not. People are far more complex than a single style type can effectively describe.

Styles give us a shorthand tool for improving our relationships if we use them properly. They help identify communication approaches that might be useful; they help match people with job assignments they will most likely enjoy and perform successfully; they help identify strategies for motivating individuals to peak performance. Perhaps the most valuable advantage of understanding personality styles is they help us be more accepting of normal differences among people.

In using any style indicator properly, it's important to remember that people are more than their temperament category. No matter which system or approach you use, be careful not to put people into "pigeon holes" based on their type. Within each type, there is a great deal of variation. People may be very strong representatives of a style or show elements of more than one. The best way to use these models in a professional context is to identify communication approaches that work for different individuals and to understand general goals and values that apply to people of a given style. When you use these models as guidelines rather than as absolutes, you can often gain helpful insight into yourself and others.

There is no such thing as a "good" or "bad" style. You'll discover in each system and each description various strengths as well as weaknesses. Because it's possible for someone to be mismatched in a particular job situation due to his or her style, you may find personality style indicators used in the hiring process. This is legitimate as long as the style indicator isn't the sole criterion used to disqualify someone.

You'll also discover that each of us finds it easier to get along with some styles than with others, and that each style has its own stress pattern. Everybody is capable of bad behavior, but the type of bad behavior we exhibit can often follow from our style. You'll discover further that a well-balanced work team often needs the special strengths and offerings of a range of different styles. While different work assignments may tap the characteristics of one style more heavily than another, the overall work to be performed often requires a combination.

How can you use style information? First, in any system you consider, learn your own style and whether you're a close or loose fit with that constellation of attributes. Do you also show strong elements of another style? Are there some styles in the model that don't describe you at all?

Depending on the complexity of the system you're using, you may be able to get an idea of the likely styles of other people, whether you can get them to complete an inventory or not. As you gain an understanding of the personality styles described, you can see them reflected in your colleagues, giving you insight about their work styles, values, and habits. By understanding their contributions, strengths, and weaknesses, you can work more effectively with others. You can communicate better with people when you approach them in terms of their style.

Tony Alessandra, in his audio program *Mastering Your Message,* refers to the "Platinum Rule": "Do unto others as *they'd* like done unto them." His assertion is that when you deal with people who possess different styles, you should alter your own behavior to fit their style if you want to achieve maximum results.

That's not as difficult—or as insincere—as it may seem at first reading. Usually the behavior adjustments occur in minor areas: talking faster or more slowly, focusing on one set of benefits rather than another, altering the level of your emotional display. Knowing how to reach people where they live makes them feel more comfortable, more validated, and more willing to open the lines of communication—a strategy that ultimately leads to effective win-win outcomes.

Finally, combine this advice with Socrates's immortal words, "Know thyself." Ideally we work to know ourselves on many levels, including how we are perceived by others and how our style and approach affect the people around us.

With a few simple concepts and tools, you have the beginnings of a great strategy for using personality styles successfully in the workplace.

Discovering Personality Styles With the *Personality Explorer*™

The *Personality Explorer*™ presented in this chapter is a quick and easy tool you can use to gain an understanding of your own work style and those around you. Although not a formally tested and validated instrument, the *Personality Explorer*™ has been developed from years of expert research to follow existing four-category style models. In most cases, it will give you outcomes close to those you'll get in other models.

Besides its advantages of speed and ease of use, the *Personality Explorer™* is attractive for several other reasons as well:

- It requires no formal psychological training.

- It can be used for both individuals and teams.

- It can be applied to a variety of work situations.

- It provides tools for improved communication.

- It enables good estimates of the styles of others, even if they don't take the test.

As with all style models, you shouldn't read too much into a particular style description here. The *Personality Explorer™* produces useful information, but certainly doesn't purport to tell you everything about someone. If you feel your style type, for example, doesn't describe you, or if you suppose someone has a particular style type but their behavior doesn't seem to confirm it, go with your observations, not the test.

Do, however, give the information a fair chance. If your style according to the test results doesn't seem to describe you, review your answers to the questions and make sure you were honest with yourself. Ask someone else who knows you well and whose opinion you trust to read the descriptions and offer some perspective. Sometimes you may be surprised in learning something new about yourself—or at least about how you appear to others.

Try completing the *Personality Explorer™* now, and then read the descriptions that follow.

The Personality Explorer™

Instructions: In each pair of response options, circle the one that best completes the sentence, "I enjoy work assignments that enable me to . . . " When you have finished, add up the circled answers in each column and place the sums in the spaces provided.

I enjoy work assignments that enable me to . . .

	A	B	C	D
1.		Know who's involved or affected	Know and understand the "why"	
2.		Be included		Be methodical
3.		Be part of a team	Be creative	
4.	Get a job done		Be creative	
5.	Be the boss	Be included		
6.	Know the goal and go to work		Know and understand the "why"	
7.	Be noticed for my accomplishments			Be noticed for my efficiency

	A	B	C	D
8.			Know and understand the "why"	Know the right way to do it
9.			Be noticed for my talents	Be noticed for my efficiency
10.	Act firmly		Perform research	
11.	Get a job done	Be part of a team		
12.			Be creative	Analyze the data
13.		Be included	Be on my own	
14.	Know the goal and go to work			Know the right way to do it
15.		Be noticed for my relationships		Be noticed for my efficiency
16.		Coordinate with others	Perform research	
17.	Be the boss			Be methodical
18.	Act firmly	Coordinate with others		
19.	Get a job done			Analyze the data

	A	B	C	D
20.	Be noticed for my accomplishments	Be noticed for my relationships		
21.			Perform research	Follow a system
22.		Be noticed for my relationships	Be noticed for my talents	
23.	Know the goal and go to work	Know who's involved or affected		
24.		Be part of a team		Analyze the data
25.		Coordinate with others		Follow a system
26.	Act firmly			Follow a system
27.	Be the boss		Be on my own	
28.		Know who's involved or affected		Know the right way to do it
29.	Be noticed for my accomplishments		Be noticed for my talents	
30.			Be on my own	Be methodical
Totals:				
	A_____	B_____	C_____	D_____

Scoring

Copy your totals into the appropriate boxes below. Your *highest* score is your primary style; your *second highest* score is your secondary style. If you have a tie for first place, both are primary styles. You'll find information on how to deal with two primary styles in the following pages.

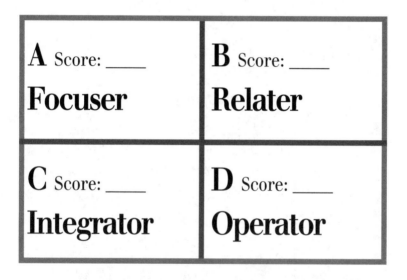

A Score: _____ **Focuser**	**B** Score: _____ **Relater**
C Score: _____ **Integrator**	**D** Score: _____ **Operator**

MY *PRIMARY* STYLE IS: _____

MY *SECONDARY* STYLE IS: _____

Interpretation of Results

The *Personality Explorer™* doesn't usually tell you anything about yourself that you don't already know. Instead, it helps you become more consciously aware of the style characteristics you possess, and how these attributes relate to the people around you.

It's important to remember not to overinterpret your score—it could vary by a few points depending on the time and circumstances under which you answered the questions. If your score is very pronounced in a certain category, it's unlikely to change very much. On the other hand, if your scores are relatively evenly distributed among the categories, you may find that circumstances will tip you from one category to another.

Similarly, when you're using this information to help you work with others, don't assume because you've learned some things about another person that you've gleaned everything there is to know. Others' scores may also be more evenly distributed, which means they may not always behave exactly as their style type may predict.

The *Personality Explorer™* represents one tool among many, not a complete set of answers in and of itself.

The following table summarizes key information about the four styles.

Personality Explorer™ Style Summary

	Focuser	Relater	Integrator	Operator
Key concern:	Focus (what)	Relate (who)	Integrate (why)	Operate (how)
Wants to know about the:	Task at hand	Big picture	Significance	Details
Preferred role:	Taking charge, working independently	Coordinating, facilitating	Problem-solving, diagnosis	Monitoring, analyzing
Values:	Practicality	Teamwork	Innovation	Documentation
Preferred management style:	Directing (authoritative)	Organizing (democratic)	Planning (self-directed)	Controlling (systematic)
Wants to be valued for being:	Productive	Flexible	Self-reliant	Accountable
Values in other people:	Successful experience	Group participation	Questioning	Compliance

Personality Explorer™ Style Summary (cont.)

	Focuser	Relater	Integrator	Operator
As a follower, respects:	Strong leadership	Group consensus and focus	Personal significance and good reasons	Policy, systems, laws, procedures
Works best when given:	Clear goals	Broad, general goals	Ideas and input	Systems
Management focus is on:	Outcomes	Involvement	Input	Procedures
Wants to have:	Authority	Influence	Time to assess	Clear boundaries
Learns best by:	Doing	Observing and participating	Listening and self-study	Repetition and procedures

Primary and Secondary Styles

As noted previously, your high score indicates your *primary style*. If your primary style is more than three points higher than any other score, you possess a definite style. You will probably find in the descriptive material that follows a clear picture of your work behavior.

Your second-place score signifies your *secondary style*. If your primary and secondary style scores fall close together (three or fewer points separating), you'll find that some parts of the secondary style description apply to you. You may have an easier time relating to people who have your secondary style as their primary style.

Because different situations call for different behaviors, you may find yourself behaving more like someone of the secondary style under certain circumstances. If your job demands characteristics of a style other than your primary one, you may find yourself acquiring some of those characteristics.

An exact tie between scores for first place doesn't mean a "split personality." Instead, you have a balance of styles. A possible advantage in close or identical scores is that you may be more flexible in your ability to understand and work with others. (However, if your score is very definite in a single style, this doesn't mean you can't be flexible; normally it suggests only that you may need to make a more conscious effort to put yourself in others' shoes.)

Some people with tied or very close style scores find that they tend to have a pronounced work style and a very different home style. Others may find that different work assignments bring out different styles. You've probably met people who seem different when they're away from work, while others stay about the same at work and at play.

You may discover changes over time. That is, styles change as we grow; they change as a reaction to circumstances; and they change based on what we need to do in our lives. If you've had the experience of attending a high school reunion, you've no doubt noticed that some people have seemingly evolved in a fairly straight line from those days to the present, while others appear to have changed quite drastically—becoming almost a different person.

It's important to emphasize that whether you have one strong style or a three-way tie, whether you've had the same style all your life or changed dramatically, neither condition is by itself abnormal or even very unusual. People exhibit a wide range of life approaches within the bounds of a style approach to personality. Value judgments like "good" (not to mention "sane") don't apply in the assignment of styles. Within each style, people can behave in ways that are productive or counterproductive—they can be easy to get along with or quite difficult, they can have an optimistic life outlook or a pessimistic one, and so on.

If you believe you may have psychological concerns, a style model will be of little relevance in helping you with them. Complete personality inventories, such as the Minnesota Multiphasic Personality Inventory (MMPI), are used in professional counseling environments in the diagnosis and treatment of potential or actual psychological problems.

Finally, a very few people may find that the style descriptions don't seem to fit. Based on experience and feedback from thousands of respondents, the *Personality Explorer*™ tends to be perceived by people who take it as accurate between 80 and 90 percent of the time. However, if none of the descriptions and categories seems to fit you, or you have a strong feeling that you belong in another category than the one assigned you, you may well be right. Try the following steps:

1. Have several people you know and trust read the style descriptions and give you feedback on how they see you. If others see you as a strong representative of your score-derived style, you may want to consider the reasons for their judgment. You may learn something very interesting about yourself.

2. If their perception confirms your own—either that none of the styles fits you or that you are in a category other than the one indicated—that perception is likely more accurate.

3. Try one or more of the other personality style indicators to see if those results parallel the *Personality Explorer*™. If other instruments give you a better fit, use them.

4. If you're someone for whom the *Personality Explorer*™ doesn't seem to work, remember that it's usefully descriptive most of the time. You can still use it effectively in your understanding of the work styles and communication preferences of others.

How to Administer the Personality Explorer™

You can use the *Personality Explorer™* instrument in a wide variety of situations, both professionally and personally. You can take it yourself, share it with family members, give copies to people in your department, or use it as a team tool. In addition to the test you've taken, there is a copy in the back of the book for you to use with teams. Permission is granted to copy the test portion only for use with members of your organization.

Why would you use the instrument? To use the *Personality Explorer™* in a professional setting, first decide on your goals and objectives: Are you trying to build team spirit? Are there communication conflicts among team members? Do you feel greater understanding of style differences will improve productivity? Do you want to know about the work style of a prospective new team member to help you get the relationship off on the best foot?

Will it help me make hiring decisions? It's not a good idea to use the *Personality Explorer™*, or any other personality style indicator, as the sole or even primary determinant for hiring or not hiring someone. In addition to possible legal issues, far more factors than style determine whether someone will be effective in a given job. It's better to use the *Personality Explorer™* as a tool for figuring out how you can work best with or communicate best with someone you've decided to hire based on merit criteria.

What's the right setting? Based on your goal, you can determine the best setting in which to administer the instrument. It can be as informal as a meeting in which you pass out copies of the test, ask people to complete it on the spot, and then discuss what the answers may mean. You can give it as a take-home exercise if it makes people more comfortable, but there is no inherent reason why the group cannot take it on the spot.

What if some people object to taking the test? It's possible that some members of a team will agree to take the test and others may protest or object. Unless you have a very compelling reason or need, it's not usually worth the conflict to make someone take this test if he or she isn't willing.

What do I do when people have taken the test? You've noticed several cautions about overinterpreting the test results and about inappropriate or judgmental uses of personality style information, and those are important. Provide information to the test takers about what styles mean and don't mean, explain that people fit their types strongly or less strongly, and remind them that style and type don't tell you everything about someone. Do everything you can to make people comfortable and unthreatened by this process.

It's useful to give people all the information as possible about their type and others—you might get multiple copies of this book, for example, to hand out to each person. Try the exercises in the book to stimulate team discussion about the types and to facilitate understanding. You'll generally find that the majority of participants really enjoy this exercise and find it quite useful in helping their understanding of others.

What about after the test period? Behavior changes and relationship changes often result from peoples' exposure to personality style information. They may be less hostile or negative about perceived behavioral problems in co-workers once they discover that the behavior is about style, not maliciousness. They may find it easier to adapt to the ways others work. Although not the cure-all for organizational woes, the communication and relationship benefits you get from administering this instrument are real.

Consider having a follow-up meeting a few months afterward, to reinforce lessons and encourage discussion about how styles and types affect the ways in which the organization, department, or team works.

Style A:
The Focuser

"I got where I am today because I get the job done," says the Focuser. The word that describes this type best is *results*. The archetypical Focuser quote is, "Winning isn't everything—it's the *only* thing!" Focusers measure their work and their lives in terms of results.

A Focuser can be merely firm and direct, or aggressive and dominant. There's a wide range of Focuser behavior, but those with this style all have in common the need for results.

Whether you're a Focuser or you work with someone who is, use the following information to improve your effectiveness.

We all encounter Focusers, who frequently find their passions move them into leadership and managerial roles. As a result, we must know how to recognize them, communicate with them, and build an effective working relationship with them. As with all the styles, you'll find that there are some with which you may have an easier or harder time relating. The key words listed below represent the positive and negative perceptions people may have of Focusers:

Positive	Negative
• Determined	• Tyrannical
• Controlled	• Domineering
• Commanding	• Dictatorial
• Authoritative	• Autocratic
• In charge	• Bossy
• Influential	• Hard-headed

Strengths of the Focuser

Focusers bring to the workplace the desire to take charge and get things done. They are practical, direct, and use authority comfortably. They focus on results and outcomes and have the drive and energy to stay on track. As a result, Focusers have a natural tendency to rise to leadership positions in any organization.

Focusers care about rules and procedures only when they help achieve desired objectives, and tend to be comfortable ignoring them when they conflict with objectives. They are at their best when goals are clearly stated and laid out, and when they are given the authority to go for them. In the absence of given authority, they tend to take authority.

Communicating With the Focuser

Focusers normally have a fast-paced communication style and can be perceived as disconcertingly direct and blunt to the other styles. Their biggest pet peeve occurs when others appear to waste their time. "Don't beat around the bush, just get to the point!" the Focuser says. To approach a Focuser, ask "What?" and "When?" questions. Sample approaches to the Focuser include the following:

- "This is what I want you to do."
- "I need five minutes of your time." (Keep your word!)
- "What do you want and when do you want it?"

If the Focuser holds a position of authority over you, you may be nervous about taking an assertive approach. You'll find in most cases that the Focuser actively likes assertiveness in staff members (but not a challenge to his or her authority). If you are clear and blunt and quick and to the point, the Focuser appreciates and understands you, and will probably respect you more.

How to Spot the Focuser

Look for fast-paced and authoritative behavior and a blunt, direct communication style. Pick up cues from the office decor. Focuser offices often demonstrate power relationships: a large desk in the middle of the office and the guest chair on the other side of the desk. Focuser offices may be busy and filled with paper but aren't usually messy and disorganized. There's generally an absence of personal decorations. Family pictures are probably on the credenza behind the desk, not on the desk itself. "Not that I don't love my family, but work is work and home is home and I know the difference!" the Focuser says.

While strong and definite Focusers are easy to spot, people whose Focuser tendencies are less pronounced may take more detective work on your part. Watch for how the person behaves under stress, for example. Focuser tendencies may rise right to the surface.

A Focuser style may include any of the others as a secondary style:

Focuser/Relater. Watch for real concern for people as individuals combined by a drive to get the work done. The Focuser/Relater may shift pace quickly depending on the situation, moving from slow-paced and relationship-oriented to fast-paced, almost brusque, when work situations require. Because these types are virtually opposite, you may have the experience of Dr. Jekyll/Mr. Hyde in dealing with them. Look for behavioral cues to find which side is currently dominant, and adapt accordingly.

Focuser/Integrator. Watch for the desk moving from busy to messy, and also notice quick changes based on new ideas. The Focuser/Integrator will tend to respond to new and exciting ideas, sometimes pushing for rapid changes in direction and then putting all the Focuser emphasis on achieving the new goals. Watch out for the tendency to ignore people and feelings in the process. It's not malicious in intent; it's simply that the Focuser/Integrator has moved past the immediate time into the future goal, and doesn't notice the immediate fallout. Focuser/Integrators often operate at high levels in the organization, where they form a common pattern—these two characteristics linked together virtually define "visionary leadership." The internal champion of new management ideas and programs, such as TQM or reengineering, is often a Focuser/Integrator, who exercises a strong leadership hand in the process.

Focuser/Operator. Watch for a driven perfectionistic style—everything must be right, all the way down to the smallest details, while still achieving broad goals. The desk, while still busy, is always well organized, and the Focuser/Operator tends to value that sort of look in your office. Focuser/Operators often feel others must meet their same perfectionistic standards, especially in areas like clean offices.

Goals of the Focuser

Understanding peoples' goals helps you understand how to work effectively with them. Focusers want more authority and power, and they feel successful when they accomplish something tangible. They want to be productive and don't understand the lack of desire for achievement or focus on productivity in other people who possess different styles.

The Focuser tends to have clear personal achievement goals and wants others on the team to support them. One key to working well with the Focuser is to know what those goals are and then show how your needs and interests can help the Focuser achieve those goals. Another key is to make your own goals very clear around a Focuser. This will help the Focuser understand you and can open the door to better communication and negotiation.

Developmental Issues for the Focuser

The Focuser does notice when people do a good job but isn't naturally inclined to praise it. After all, the Focuser feels this is the natural way people are (or should be). When people do something wrong, however, it's a different story. To increase your effectiveness as a supervisor if you're a Focuser, you need to work at recognizing the strengths of others, listening better, and gaining support. Sometimes, without intending to do so, the Focuser can leave resentment, anger, and frustration in his or her wake.

Focusers need to work on teamwork, especially if they are strong representatives of their type (preferring traditional authority relationships and clearly defined power). If their interests and needs aren't met, Focusers will often work against the interests of the team, believing that one person's clear leadership is a better strategy for success.

Stress Style of the Focuser

Under stress, the Focuser can become impulsive, hot-tempered, demanding, and dictatorial. All these are exaggerations of normal style and show the extent of frustration. Some Focusers may choose to live in the extreme elements of their style, becoming classic "difficult people." Yelling, bullying, demanding, and even physically aggressive actions can result.

The Focuser in Other Systems

While each personality style system approaches the types somewhat differently, following are the closest analogs to the Personality Explorer's Focuser:

System	Type
Albrecht	Blue Sky
Alessandra ("Platinum Rule")	Director
Atkins	Controlling Taking
DeVille	Controller
Hippocrates	Choleric
Jung	Sensor
Lefton	Quadrant 1 Dominant/ Hostile
Myers-Briggs	ESTJ, ESTP, ENTJ, ENTP
PPS/DiSC	D – Dominance
Smalley	Lion
TEAM (Temme)	Targeted/Boss
Wilson, Tracom, Merrill	Driver

My Focuser Score: _____

Exercise:
Focusers I Know and Work With

▼

Person 1: _____

Focuser Characteristics:

_____

_____

_____

_____

_____

_____

Strategies for Working Better With That Person:

_____

_____

_____

_____

_____

_____

_____

Person 2: _____

Focuser Characteristics:

_____

_____

_____

_____

_____

_____

Strategies for Working Better With That Person:

_____

_____

_____

_____

_____

_____

Person 3: _____

Focuser Characteristics:

_____

_____

_____

_____

_____

_____

Strategies for Working Better With That Person:

_____

_____

_____

_____

_____

_____

Style B:
The Relater

"I succeed because of the team," says the Relater. "I got where I am today because I build good relationships and make sure that people are taken care of." As the name suggests, the word that describes Relaters best is *relationships.* The archetypical Relater concern, in the words of Dale Carnegie, is "how to win friends and influence people." Relaters measure their work and their lives in terms of the quality of their relationships with others.

A Relater can simply have a strong concern for other people, or this type can be unassertive and inappropriately giving. There is a wide range of Relater behavior, but Relaters all have in common a concern for how others feel in general— and specifically how others feel about them.

Whether you're a Relater or you work with Relaters, use the information that follows to improve your effectiveness.

We all work with Relaters in roles ranging from staff positions to leadership. While Relaters don't have the driving passion of, say, a Focuser for a leadership position, they're often selected for leadership roles because of their people skills, especially when those people skills are balanced with personal assertiveness. As with all types, it's important that you learn how to recognize Relaters, communicate with them, and build an effective working relationship with them. Building a relationship with a Relater can be easy, but sometimes it takes a special effort to make it effective in the workplace.

As with all the styles, you'll find that there are some with which you may have an easier or harder time relating. The key words in the chart that follows represent some of the positive and negative perceptions people may have of Relaters.

Positive	Negative
• Listener	• Unassertive
• Caring	• Too personal
• Team player	• Goes along
• Loyal	• Slavish
• Friendly	• Gushing
• Sympathetic	• Indecisive

Strengths of the Relater

Relaters bring to the workplace the ability to facilitate teams, to get groups of people working together to achieve common goals. Their management style is democratic, they are generally good listeners, and they demonstrate their caring through their regular behavior.

Relaters make excellent managers in organizations that have a team focus because of the priority they put on people. They are often willing to make exceptions to rules and procedures based on individual circumstances and issues. They work hard to build consensus and to make others feel involved in pursuing company objectives. They are at their best in organizations that value team building and team efforts and that demonstrate concern and compassion for people.

Communicating With the Relater

Relaters usually have an indirect communication style and are slower-paced. (Note that "pace" is not synonymous with "accomplishment"; some fast-paced people spin their wheels. And don't forget that it was the tortoise, not the hare, who won the big race.) Relaters don't trust ideas, they trust people. They need to get to know you as a person. "Come in, have a cup of tea, and let's get to know each other," says this personality type.

Relaters often have a strong need for inclusion, so make them feel like they're part of what you're doing. Sometimes they have difficulty saying "no," but don't mistake that for being a pushover. Relaters can be quite stubborn, but they are polite and understanding as they refuse. "Who?" and "What else?" questions are useful in communicating with Relaters. Some good approaches to use include the following:

- "I would like your opinion."
- "I need your help."
- "Can we talk about _____ together?"
- "Let's discuss some options for _____."

If the Relater holds a position of authority over you, it's important that you demonstrate concern for people issues in your communication approaches. If you are a naturally fast-paced person, take some time. Relaters are more concerned with the best decision than with a rapid one. If you're faced with a Relater who's having trouble making a decision, show empathy and a willingness to compromise in order to get better support.

Relaters need to be valued as human beings, whatever their role or level in an organization. Demonstrate a reasonable amount of concern for their personal lives, their families, and similar issues. Simple touches, like remembering names of spouses, children, and pets, remembering birthdays, and asking follow-up questions about important life issues and known interests and concerns, can make a significant improvement in your dealings with a Relater.

How to Spot the Relater

Look for a slower-paced communication style and lots of involvement with people. The Relater's office is often home-like. Ideally, the Relater's desk is against the wall, not in the middle of the room, so he or she doesn't have to look at you across the desk—it's so cold and distancing. Relaters' offices have lots of personal photographs, drawings from their children, and possibly flowers on their desk. Some go so far as to bring in their own lamps from home (fluorescent light is so cold!).

While strong and definite Relaters are easy to spot, identifying people whose Relater tendencies are less pronounced may take more detective work on your part. Watch for how the person behaves under stress, for example. Relater tendencies may rise right to the surface.

A Relater style also may include any of the other styles as a secondary style:

Relater/Focuser. The Relater with Focuser characteristics starts with a strong concern for people and their interests and balances it with a drive to get the work done. The

Relater/Focuser is more fast-paced than the strong Relater, but always has time for people issues *when they relate to the work to be accomplished.* Even under stress, the Relater/Focuser tends to be a good listener. The difference between a Relater/Focuser and a Focuser/Relater may be subtle. Under stress, the person may retreat to the extremes of his or her primary style, or have oddly timed lapses into Relater behavior when Focuser behavior is called for.

Relater/Integrator. When you combine the people orientation of the Relater with the idea focus of the Integrator, you get a Relater with a great deal of enthusiasm. Instead of ideas being valued in and of themselves, as in the case of the Integrator, Relater/Integrators value ideas primarily as they relate to people: how to make them happy, productive, and successful within the confines of the organizational mission. Watch for problems in coming to closure and finishing major initiatives.

Relater/Operator. The Relater/Operator is very slow-paced in style and combines the people concerns of the Relater with the detail-oriented concerns of the Operator. The Relater/Operator may focus extensively on training in procedures and in detailed oversight of the work. One hallmark of the Relater/Operator style is *patience.* Watch out for difficulties in decision making, especially when all the data is not available, and for indecisiveness under pressure.

Goals of the Relater

Understanding people's goals helps you understand how to work effectively with them. The Relater wants inclusion, wants to be liked, and wants to facilitate teamwork.

Consensus is an important goal for the Relater, who is uncomfortable with disagreement and conflict, especially when it becomes negative and charged.

The Relater is most comfortable with people with whom he or she can relate. To succeed in your relationships with Relaters, you must be one of those people. Fortunately, it's not hard, since Relaters are also working toward the same goal. As noted, make sure you notice and ask about personal issues on a regular basis, remember names of important people in the Relater's life, and show a concern for the Relater as an individual and a human being.

Developmental Issues for the Relater

The Relater needs to work on task focus and sometimes on personal assertiveness. While personal relationships are legitimate and important in the workplace, sometimes the role of the supervisor requires a willingness to be disliked. Accepting some negative feelings on the part of others is an important challenge for the Relater.

Another good area for Relater development is negotiation skills. While becoming a better negotiator is a worthwhile goal for everyone, the "win/win" negotiation style presented in venues such as the Harvard Negotiation Project's *Getting to Yes* and Stephen Covey's *The Seven Habits of Highly Effective People* fits the pro-people/pro-relationship needs of the Relater and yet points the path to assertive solutions that support the Relater's needs and goals in the workplace.

Stress Style of the Relater

Under stress, the Relater can become overly emotional, have difficulty making decisions, or take on too much responsibility in an effort not to hurt anybody. As the stress continues to mount and the Relater finds that he or she cannot please everyone, this personality type can become critical, flippant, and rebellious. "Why do I have to do everything around here?" the stressed-out Relater cries.

Relaters who choose to live in the extreme elements of their style become classic "difficult people." They may work to avoid decisions at all costs, leaving many important issues unresolved because of their extreme unwillingness to confront any unpleasantness. Alternatively, they may say "yes" to everything, only to neglect it later because of their hyper desire to please.

The Relater in Other Systems

While each personality style system approaches the types somewhat differently, following are the closest analogs to the Personality Explorer's™ Relater:

System	Type
Albrecht	Red Earth
Alessandra ("Platinum Rule")	Relater
Atkins	Supporting Giving
DeVille	Supporter
Hippocrates	Phlegmatic
Jung	Feeler
Lefton Warm	Quadrant 3, Submissive
Myers-Briggs	ISFJ, ISFP, ENFJ, ENFP
PPS/DiSC	S – Steadiness
Smalley	Golden Retriever
TEAM (Temme)	Accommodating/ Cheerleader
Wilson, Tracom, Merrill	Amiable

My Relater Score: _____

Exercise:
Relaters I Know and Work With

▼

Person 1: _____

Relater Characteristics:

_____

_____

_____

_____

_____

_____

Strategies for Working Better With That Person:

_____

_____

_____

_____

_____

_____

Person 2: _____

Relater Characteristics:

_____

_____

_____

_____

_____

_____

Strategies for Working Better With That Person:

_____

_____

_____

_____

_____

_____

Person 3: _____

Relater Characteristics:

_____

_____

_____

_____

_____

_____

Strategies for Working Better With That Person:

_____

_____

_____

_____

_____

_____

Style C:
The Integrator

"I can do anything as long as it makes sense to me," says the Integrator. "I analyze the problem, brainstorm the options, construct a model, and make it happen. The secret of success is to ask good questions." The word that describes the Integrator best is *ideas*. The archetypical Integrator quote is, "Why don't we brainstorm for awhile and see what we find out!" Integrators live in the future more than in the present, and believe the world is full of exciting options just waiting to be explored!

An Integrator can be positively future-directed and possibility oriented, or this type can be full of impractical ideas and no consistent direction. Though there's a wide range of Integrator behavior, they all have in common the need for *new ideas*. For an Integrator, the idea is the important thing—the implementation often becomes a secondary matter.

Whether you're an Integrator or just work with them, use the information that follows to improve your effectiveness.

Many Integrators find themselves in leadership roles. They are often in charge of projects, teams, and task forces, because of the strength, energy, and frequency of their ideas and because of the enthusiasm they bring to almost any endeavor. Integrators are also often found in technical roles as computer programmers, engineers, and product designers and in similar pursuits where they can develop their ideas and bring them to fruition.

As a result, you must know how to recognize Integrators, communicate with them, and build an effective working relationship with them. As with all the styles, you'll find that there are some with which you may have an easier or harder time relating. The key words that follow represent the positive and negative perceptions people may have of Integrators.

Positive	Negative
• Imaginative	• Impractical
• Creative	• Unrealistic
• Energetic	• Manic
• Brainstormers	• Time-wasters
• Future-directed	• Head in the clouds
• Multi-tasking	• Unable to finish
• Persuasive	• Con artists

Strengths of the Integrator

Integrators are the "Why?" people, experts in problem solving, idea generation, innovation, and strategic planning. Skilled model builders and analysts, Integrators focus on the future, on long-range and strategic issues, policies, and in-depth analysis. The person who understands the latest management models, the advanced techniques, is usually an Integrator. They are never afraid to venture into unknown territory, trusting on creativity, innovation, and their own ability to get them through.

For Integrators, the most important element of rules and procedures is that they make logical sense. If they don't make sense, it's very difficult for the Integrator to take them seriously. On the other hand, an Integrator is seldom likely to violate rules just for the sake of it; if there is no good reason to do otherwise, an Integrator is likely to follow procedures so as not to waste time.

Communicating With the Integrator

Integrators, like Focusers, are fast-paced communicators, capable of passion and excitement about ideas. They love to hear who else has used it, what the results were, and how new an idea it is. Ideas and options are naturally exciting to them. Be careful: an Integrator's enthusiasm is not necessarily agreement. This type is quite capable of loving your idea for its creativity and still rejecting it because it doesn't fit the mission. "That was brilliant," the Integrator may say. "Completely wrong, but brilliant."

Even when the Integrator is very positive about your idea or concept, he or she may still challenge you. Don't be insulted or fearful; that's just the Integrator probing to make sure the idea is fully sound and defensible. "Why?" and "What else?" questions are powerful tools for working with the Integrator. Good approaches to use with the Integrator include the following:

- "What do you think about _____?"
- "I would like your ideas and input on _____."
- "Would you help me brainstorm some ideas about this problem?"
- "What alternatives can you think of about _____?"

If the Integrator holds a position of authority over you, you may be intimidated by his or her fast-moving mind and feel that if your style is more methodical or slow-paced, you are somehow deficient. Generally, Integrators are very tolerant and accepting of how other people work, but when they don't possess a lot of Relater characteristics, they may omit the social niceties and make you feel stupid or wrong when they don't necessarily intend to do that at all.

How to Spot the Integrator

Look for a fast-paced style, lots of "Why?" questions, and an enjoyment of ideas and brainstorming for its own sake. Also, look in the office for clues. The classic Integrator office is chaos personified. "A clean desk is the sign of a sick mind," the Integrator says jokingly, but the office stays chaotic because the Integrator is thinking about six different things at once, most of them far in the future, and cleaning the desk seems mundane and nonproductive. "Why spend my time on this? I know where everything is, anyway . . . well, mostly," the Integrator says.

While strong and definite Integrators are easy to spot, identifying people whose Integrator tendencies are less pronounced may take more detective work on your part. Watch for how the person behaves under stress, for example. Integrator tendencies may rise right to the surface.

An Integrator style may also have any of the other styles as a secondary style:

Integrator/Focuser. This is a fairly common pattern, and one you may often find in strong leadership roles in the organization, because these two characteristics linked together virtually define "visionary leadership." The internal champion of new management ideas, from TQM to reengineering, is usually an Integrator/Focuser. The stylistic difference between the Integrator/Focuser and the Focuser/ Integrator is that the former emphasizes ideas more and the latter emphasizes results more. Both are fast-paced styles, leading to an extremely fast-talking, fast-thinking, fast-paced individual.

Integrator/Relater. When the Integrator personality is combined with Relater characteristics, you find enthusiasm tempered by more concerns for the needs, ideas, and wishes of other people. Integrators are not naturally strong listeners, so the Relater listening skills help in this regard. The impact of ideas on people are of more concern to the Integrator/ Relater, and often ideas *about* people and how they work best are the focus of the Integrator/Relater's brainstorming talents.

Integrator/Operator. This idea and detail combination is often powerful in occupations where both are necessary, such as many disciplines of engineering. Integrator/ Operators are systems thinkers: how does it work, how do the pieces fit together, and how can it be streamlined and organized for maximum efficiency? Again, beware of the tendency to admire the system for its own sake, rather than for what it accomplishes.

Goals of the Integrator

Understanding people's goals helps you understand how to work effectively with them. The Integrator wants to be appreciated for imagination, intelligence, creativity, insight, and talent. Integrators like to be noticed for their own characteristics. The Integrator often prefers to be self-directed—rather than part of a team—and may assume you also prefer to be left alone (which may or may not suit your style). Integrators have clear personal goals and work toward them. Stylistically, they are sprinters, not marathoners, capable of amazing amounts of work in short periods of time, followed by periods in which they seem to accomplish little.

Integrators can be people-oriented or not. People-oriented Integrators can while away pleasant hours in endless meetings that discuss ideas, policies, new directions. Non-people-oriented Integrators like people best when they serve as an audience for their monologues.

The Integrator is most comfortable with people who show respect and admiration for his or her ideas, and you need to be one of those people to make the relationship successful. You don't have to agree with or accept the validity of an Integrator's idea; you just have to admire its creativity and uniqueness. (That's an odd concept for some of the other styles to accept, but it's often the best way to end a conversation with an Integrator when you don't agree. "That's really creative," you can say, and you'll be surprised how much more acceptable it is when you disagree.

Developmental Issues for the Integrator

The Integrator's long-range focus is useful, but sometimes short-term focus and immediate small issues are important as well. The Integrator needs to work on being organized in the small details, balancing the work effort rather than always sprinting, and keeping the chaos within reasonable boundaries. With other people, the Integrator needs to realize that others don't always find the same value in ideas for their own sake, and instead value certainty and predictability over imagination and excitement.

An Integrator sometimes needs more grounding in reality, accepting organizational and human limitations. Often an Integrator needs to develop more sensitivity to when others have had enough brainstorming and are ready to go to work, or when others are tired of listening to the Integrator's enthusiasm about the latest great idea.

Stress Style of the Integrator

Under stress, the Integrator can sometimes just give up. "Fine! If you people don't want to improve or change, that's okay. Call me when you're ready to do something useful," the Integrator says scornfully. This type can become impatient or even insulting about the intellectual or creative deficiencies of other people. Sometimes the Integrator, who has such a clear vision of the future, becomes uncommunicative, withdrawn, and depressed when no progress seems to be occurring. Everything seems futile.

Another characteristic of the Integrator under stress is lack of follow-through. The messy desk so often characteristic of this person comes from focusing on the excitement of the newest idea and dropping old ideas by the wayside to be finished "whenever." This results in nothing getting accomplished, and lots of energy expended toward that result.

When Integrators feel on the defensive or attacked, they continue to passionately defend their ideas, even if it's clear to everyone (including the Integrator, secretly) that it's hopelessly impractical. This happens most often when the idea is attacked before the Integrator's creativity is acknowledged. To help an Integrator get out of this cycle, say nice things about the creativity and imagination that produced the idea, and how it might lead to new insights—then talk about any ways the idea won't quite work in reality.

The Integrator in Other Systems

While each personality style system approaches the types somewhat differently, following are the closest analogs to the Personality Explorer's™ Integrator:

System	Type
Albrecht	Red Sky
Alessandra ("Platinum Rule")	Socializer
Atkins	Adapting dealing
DeVille	Entertainer
Hippocrates	Sanguine
Jung	Intuitor
Lefton	Quadrant 4 Dominant/ Warm
Myers-Briggs	INTJ, INTP, INFJ, INFP
PPS/DiSC	I – Influencing
Smalley	Otter
TEAM (Temme)	Enthusiastic/Champion
Wilson, Tracom, Merrill	Expressive

My Integrator Score: _____

Exercise:
Integrators I Know and Work With

▼

Person 1: _____

Integrator Characteristics:

_____

_____

_____

_____

_____

_____

Strategies for Working Better With That Person:

_____

_____

_____

_____

_____

_____

Person 2: _____

Integrator Characteristics:

_____

_____

_____

_____

_____

_____

Strategies for Working Better With That Person:

_____

_____

_____

_____

_____

_____

Person 3: _____

Integrator Characteristics:

_____

_____

_____

_____

_____

_____

Strategies for Working Better With That Person:

_____

_____

_____

_____

_____

_____

Style D:
The Operator

"My ability to stay organized and to ensure that the details are under control lies at the core of my success," says the Operator. "I make a plan that is detailed and thorough. I make sure the process is systematic, well-documented, and in compliance with policy. As long as the process is correctly followed, the desired results are obtained."

An Operator can simply be detail-oriented and thorough, or can become compulsive and perfectionistic. There's a wide range of Operator behavior, but all Operators have in common a focus on *details* and *process*. For an Operator, it's not enough to get the right result—it must be acheived using the proper process as well.

Whether you're an Operator or you work with them, use the information that follows to improve your effectiveness.

Operators are found in management roles—less often in leadership positions—when details and process management are the critical ingredients for success. Operators also hold a variety of staff positions in such areas as accounting, quality assurance, and technical support, where their strengths are essential. As a result, we must know how to recognize them, communicate with them, and build an effective working relationship with them.

As with all the styles, you'll find that there are some with which you may have an easier or harder time relating. The key words in the chart that follows represent the positive and negative perceptions people may have of Operators.

Positive	Negative
• Detailed	• Obsessive
• Procedural	• Rigid
• Accurate	• Finicky
• Organized	• Compulsively neat
• Methodical	• Slow
• Correct	• Nitpicking
• Fact-oriented	• Visionless

Strengths of the Operator

Operators bring to the workplace a sense of detail. The "how" of a process is most important to them. Operators are therefore skilled at documenting, controlling, systematizing, and accounting. They are the masters of minutiae, procedures, and boundaries. When the work can be well-defined and the quality lies in the details, the Operator is in his or her element.

For Operators, rules and procedures are ends in themselves, and conformity to them is an important and legitimate goal. It takes an exceptional reason to cause an Operator to choose not to follow a rule or a procedure, and he or she is likely to take care that either the procedure is subsequently modified or the exception well-documented.

Communicating With the Operator

Operators have an indirect and task-oriented style. They are slower-paced, which is part of their methodical approach, and they can be perceived as too detail-oriented by the other styles. They are frustrated when others seem not to respect the rules, policies, procedures, and systems that are set up to manage the work.

When communicating with an Operator, emphasize how what you want fits the system and the policy. Show your respect for details and accuracy. Avoid hyperbolic language ("You never . . . " "This is the worst . . . ")—be precise and factual when you describe a problem. "How?" and "Where?" questions are very useful with the Operator. Try such phrases as the following:

- "How would you do this?"
- "Here's how to proceed. First, _____. Second, _____. Third, _____."
- "Our priorities have changed. Here are the facts."
- "I need five minutes. When would be a good time?"
- "What additional information do you need before you make a decision?"

If the Operator holds a position of authority over you, you may be frustrated by someone whom you perceive to work too slowly or be unable to make a decision, or intimidated by what you may see as an extremely analytical and fault-finding style. Generally, Operators start by being distrustful of other people's work, which is a consequence of the detail orientation.

A lack of trust about your work isn't intended as a personal attack or as a reflection on your competency. Instead, it's like auditing the books. You perform an audit not because you think your accountants are incompetent or dishonest; you audit because it's a good check and balance, a way to catch errors, a means to identify opportunity for improvement. Auditing and checking your work is intended for the same reasons. The first strategy is to accept the Operator's auditing style for what it is rather than interpreting it in light of your own style.

The next strategy to follow with the Operator is to develop a reputation for attention to detail yourself. The worst thing you can do with this type is try to hurry him or her through the evaluation process. This will likely cause the Operator to think you're trying to hide something. If you show patience and support for his or her style, the Operator will grow in trust of you. Over time, he or she will feel less need to double- and triple-check your work, and you'll get faster decisions.

How to Spot the Operator

Look for slow-paced, methodical behavior and strong attention to detail. The office decor of the Operator often reflects the personality. Look for a well-organized and neat desk, charts and timelines posted on the wall, and a sense that everything has an exact place. Operator offices are often modest and plain; they don't need the official trappings of rank.

While strong and definite Operators are easy to spot, identifying people whose Operator tendencies are less pronounced may take more detective work on your part. Watch for how the person behaves under stress, for example. Operator tendencies may rise right to the surface.

An Operator style may also have any of the others as a secondary style:

Operator/Focuser. When the primary Operator style is combined with strong Focuser tendencies, you'll find a more driven perfectionist, someone who expects details *and* results. This style is moderately paced and tends to be authoritarian. The desk, while still busy, is always well-organized, and the Operator/Focuser tends to care that your office also looks appropriate.

Operator/Relater. The Operator/Relater is very slow-paced in style, and combines the detail-oriented concerns of the Operator with the people and relationship concerns of the Relater. This combination makes an ideal staff support person, and you may find this type looking for a mentor or leader for whom he or she can provide support.

Operator/Integrator. The Operator/Integrator is a system-oriented thinker with a primary orientation to detail. This combination is best at taking and developing ideas, writing detailed reports, preparing organizational charts, and providing project management documentation. This person is powerful in project-related positions. The Operator/Integrator makes an excellent #2 on a project team.

Goals

Understanding people's goals helps you understand how to work effectively with them. The Operator values being part of the system and doing the right thing at all times. He or she feels most comfortable working inside established procedures, conforming to policy, and not calling unnecessary attention to him- or herself. He or she may be happiest when assignments are clear-cut, with a right way and a wrong way to do them. These individuals value being praised for their precision, detail, and loyalty.

Operators are made uncomfortable by too much emotion displayed on the job, including too much excitement and enthusiasm. They are often distrustful of "grand schemes," finding the devil in the details.

Developmental Issues for the Operator

The Operator may have a tendency toward perfectionism, sometimes following the rules and procedures even when it's obvious they will not yield the desired results. Operators must learn to accept variance from established norms as long as the variance stays within acceptable limits (i.e., there's usually more than one right and acceptable way to do the work). The Operator may also need to learn that people who aren't detail-oriented also can achieve acceptable results, although in a very different manner.

The Operator must learn to identify the purpose and goal in projects and systems, and focus his or her detail sense where it will be most productive for the organization. By doing so, the Operator can also learn when to let things slide by, and when rules and procedures can be legitimately modified or temporarily put aside.

Stress Style of the Operator

Under stress, the Operator can become suspicious, and the lack of trust characteristic of the style goes to extremes. Whenever someone isn't doing something exactly according to policy and established procedure, the stressed-out Operator may believe that the person is deliberately violating the rules and creating problems. Operators also can become nit-picking perfectionists and absolutely stubborn about procedures, even when protocol doesn't matter.

Operators under stress can also become compulsive about trivia, avoiding primary areas of responsibility—especially ones with "fuzzy" characteristics—in favor of smaller areas they can rigidly control.

The Operator in Other Systems

While each personality style system approaches the types somewhat differently, following are the closest analogs to the Personality Explorer's™ Operator:

System	Type
Albrecht	Blue Earth
Alessandra ("Platinum Rule")	Thinker
Atkins	Conserving Holding
DeVille	Comprehender
Hippocrates	Melancholic
Jung	Thinker
Lefton	Quadrant 2 Submissive/ Hostile
Myers-Briggs	ISTJ, ISTP, ESFJ, ESFP
PPS/DiSC	C – Cautiousness
Smalley	Beaver
TEAM (Temme)	Meditative/Doer
Wilson, Tracom, Merrill	Analytical

My Operator Score: _____

Exercise:
Operators I Know and Work With

▼

Person 1: _____

Operator Characteristics:

_____

_____

_____

_____

_____

Strategies for Working Better With That Person:

_____

_____

_____

_____

_____

Person 2: _____

Operator Characteristics:

_____

_____

_____

_____

_____

_____

Strategies for Working Better With That Person:

_____

_____

_____

_____

_____

_____

Person 3: _____

Operator Characteristics:

_____

_____

_____

_____

_____

_____

Strategies for Working Better With That Person:

_____

_____

_____

_____

_____

_____

Working Within the Style Spectrum

In organizations of any size, we normally work with people exhibiting degrees of all four *Personality Explorer™* styles. You'll often discover that a number of the people with whom you have problems, whether managers or team members, share the same style. Your challenge is to improve your own flexibility so that you can relate to others in the style they find easiest to accept. This will help you work more effectively with them.

The *Personality Explorer™* and most other four-quadrant models tend to group people by two observable behavioral characteristics: direct/indirect behavior and task/people behavior. To improve your relationships with others, move your behavior in their direction. The following model and descriptive text should supply you with many ideas.

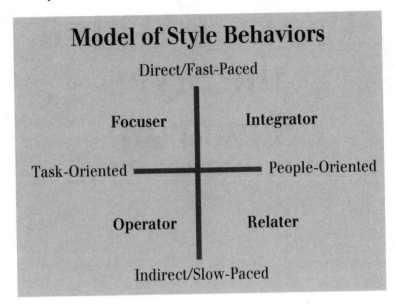

Model of Style Behaviors

Direct/Fast-Paced

Focuser   Integrator

Task-Oriented ━━━━╋━━━━ People-Oriented

Operator   Relater

Indirect/Slow-Paced

Direct/Fast-Paced. People who are direct and fast-paced tend to say what they mean, speak up at meetings, and be more naturally assertive. They speak at a faster rate, move at a faster rate, and make decisions at a faster rate. Instead of waiting for a break in the conversation, direct people are more likely to interrupt or "talk on top of" the other speakers.

To relate to direct/fast-paced people, speed up your own communication style. Don't think of yourself as interrupting; think of the dialogue as consisting of mid-air handoffs. Say what you mean and get to the point in the first sentence.

Indirect/Slow-Paced. People who are indirect and slow-paced tend not to speak out at meetings and in public settings. They often listen first and talk second. Instead of getting right to the point, they may provide background first. They tend to wait until there is a real gap in the conversation before speaking up.

To relate to indirect and slow-paced people, slow down your own communication style. Watch for clues that a person wants to speak and give them a definite pause that constitutes permission to join in. Ask them for their opinion. Provide background information before coming to your main point. Lay the foundation for what you're planning to say.

Task-Oriented. Task-oriented people tend to show their emotions less and tend to focus their behavior, actions, and choices on the tasks and goals before them rather than on the relationships and people around them.

To relate better to task-oriented people, start by identifying the tasks and goals to be achieved. Phrase your goals and interests in terms of these tasks and goals. Show less obvious emotional behavior, whether positive or negative (it doesn't matter). Use more restrained hand gestures, and speak in an even voice.

People-Oriented. People-oriented individuals tend to express their emotional reactions and feelings more easily and openly, and they regard the work environment as involving relationships as well as tasks and duties.

To relate better to people-oriented types, express how you *feel* about what's going on as well as what's *actually* going on. Ask about the feelings of the others in the conversation. Ask about personal issues as well as professional issues. Show good manners and courteous behavior (think customer service—after all, customers can be internal as well as external).

Based on the model, you'll notice that the four styles (Focuser, Relater, Integrator, Operator) correspond to the various quadrants (Direct/Fast-Paced, Indirect/Slow-Paced, Task-Oriented, People-Oriented) in the following way:

Focuser   Direct/Fast-Paced and Task-Oriented

Relater   Indirect/Slow-Paced and People-Oriented

Integrator   Direct/Fast-Paced and People-Oriented

Operator   Indirect/Slow-Paced and Task-Oriented

You'll normally experience the greatest challenges working either with your opposing style (Focuser–Relater or Integrator–Operator) or with your own style in other people. In working with your opposing style, work on altering the amount of concern you demonstrate for either people or task, as appropriate, and the pace and directness in your approach. In working with your own style in other people, move toward the center, or else both of you will tend to move toward the extremes of your style.

Identifying Style Characteristics in Others

For you to get the best use of the ideas and techniques in this book, practice your observation skills so that you become comfortable identifying style characteristics in others. The following suggestions make good practice, because you can apply them to people you know and gain insight and improved relationships while you learn.

For example, keep a behavior observation log for a few days. Observe how others act in meetings and other office situations and list types of behavior that fit the description of direct and indirect behaviors. Photocopy these sheets, if necessary, to give yourself room to work.

Maintain four sections in your log, covering each of the behavior types. Pick several people to observe, and note behavior that fits into the four quadrants. Do you see regular patterns of behavior that correspond to the *Personality Explorer™?*

You may find it advisable to record your notes privately, or make sure others know what you're doing—and why. Alternatively, if you're working with the *Personality Explorer™* in a team setting, get everyone involved in this effort and see what you learn together. The following log provides a sample format.

Behavior Log

Section 1: Director

Person   Observed Direct and Task
Behavior

_____   _____

_____   _____

_____   _____

_____   _____

_____   _____

_____   _____

Section 2: Relater

Person   Observed Indirect and People
Behavior

_____   _____

_____   _____

_____   _____

_____   _____

_____   _____

_____   _____

Section 3: Integrator

Person   Observed Direct and People
Behavior

_____   _____

_____   _____

_____   _____

_____   _____

_____   _____

_____   _____

Section 4: Operator

Person   Observed Indirect and Task
Behavior

_____   _____

_____   _____

_____   _____

_____   _____

_____   _____

_____   _____

After you've made these observations, see if you can identify regular styles of behavior. For each of the people you've been observing, can you now fit them into the *Personality Explorer™* types? Are they strong examples of their type, or is their behavior mixed?

Person	Observed Behavior Type	Strong/Weak/Mixed
_____	_____	_____
_____	_____	_____
_____	_____	_____
_____	_____	_____
_____	_____	_____
_____	_____	_____

Besides the behavior log, certain other activities (which follow) can help you better understand how the various styles operate in common workplace situations. They also make great group activities if you're working with the *Personality Explorer™* in a team environment. The important element here is not the actual, specific answers you come up with; it's the work you put into it. By thinking of the types and their behaviors, you gain valuable insight you can use for daily application.

Exercise:

▼

1. How would each type give a job assignment?

Focuser: _____

_____

_____

_____

Relater: _____

_____

_____

_____

Integrator: _____

_____

_____

_____

Operator: _____

_____

_____

_____

2. How would each type react to a major change in policy?

Focuser: _____

_____

_____

_____

Relater: _____

_____

_____

_____

Integrator: _____

_____

_____

_____

Operator: _____

_____

_____

_____

3. How would each type choose a pet?

Focuser: _____

_____

_____

_____

Relater: _____

_____

_____

_____

Integrator: _____

_____

_____

_____

Operator: _____

_____

_____

_____

4. How would each type behave if the building caught on fire?

Focuser: _____

_____

_____

_____

Relater: _____

_____

_____

_____

Integrator: _____

_____

_____

_____

Operator: _____

_____

_____

_____

5. How would each type shop for a major appliance?

Focuser: _____

_____

_____

_____

Relater: _____

_____

_____

_____

Integrator: _____

_____

_____

_____

Operator: _____

_____

_____

_____

6. What would be the perfect job situation for each
type?

Focuser: _____

_____

_____

_____

Relater: _____

_____

_____

_____

Integrator: _____

_____

_____

_____

Operator: _____

_____

_____

_____

7. What would be the perfect vacation for each type?

Focuser: _____

_____

_____

_____

Relater: _____

_____

_____

_____

Integrator: _____

_____

_____

_____

Operator: _____

_____

_____

_____

Once you have determined your own *Personality Explorer™* type, and perhaps administered the instrument to your colleagues and team members (or used the descriptions to get an idea of their likely types), you can continuously use the style information to improve your communication and management effectiveness.

Tackle some of the following questions, either by yourself or as a team, to keep your acquired skills and insights fresh:

- Consider how your style relates to the style of each member of your team. Is it the same style, or a different one? Where are your styles likely to support each other? Where are they likely to conflict?

_____

_____

_____

- Think about current relationships among people on your team. Where has there been conflict and where have people gotten along naturally very well? How do the style characteristics of each person affect the relationships? Now that you've discussed some style differences, is it easier to communicate with or understand some of those with whom you've previously had conflict?

_____

_____

_____

- Keep the styles in mind as you work for the next few weeks. Are you able to predict how people will react to certain situations or requests? Try some of the tips offered in earlier chapters about approaching people within the context of their own style. Does it feel natural to you? Does it change the response you get?

_____

_____

_____

_____

- The next time you find yourself in a conflict situation with team members, consider their styles and your own. What kinds of adjustments could you make that would help them feel more supported and acknowledged? How did they react when you tried those changes?

_____

_____

_____

The Personality Explorer™

Instructions: In each pair of response options, circle the one that best completes the sentence, "I enjoy work assignments that enable me to . . . " When you have finished, add up the circled answers in each column and place the sums in the spaces provided.

	A	B	C	D
	I enjoy work assignments that enable me to . . .			
1.		Know who's involved or affected	Know and understand the "why"	
2.		Be included		Be methodical
3.		Be part of a team	Be creative	
4.	Get a job done		Be creative	
5.	Be the boss	Be included		
6.	Know the goal and go to work		Know and understand the "why"	
7.	Be noticed for my accomplishments			Be noticed for my efficiency

	A	B	C	D
8.			Know and understand the "why"	Know the right way to do it
9.			Be noticed for my talents	Be noticed for my efficiency
10.	Act firmly		Perform research	
11.	Get a job done	Be part of a team		
12.			Be creative	Analyze the data
13.		Be included	Be on my own	
14.	Know the goal and go to work			Know the right way to do it
15.		Be noticed for my relationships		Be noticed for my efficiency
16.		Coordinate with others	Perform research	
17.	Be the boss			Be methodical
18.	Act firmly	Coordinate with others		
19.	Get a job done			Analyze the data

A	B	C	D
20. Be noticed for my accomplishments	Be noticed for my relationships		
21.		Perform research	Follow a system
22.	Be noticed for my relationships	Be noticed for my talents	
23. Know the goal and go to work	Know who's involved or affected		
24.	Be part of a team		Analyze the data
25.	Coordinate with others		Follow a system
26. Act firmly			Follow a system
27. Be the boss		Be on my own	
28.	Know who's involved or affected		Know the right way to do it
29. Be noticed for my accomplishments		Be noticed for my talents	
30.		Be on my own	Be methodical

Totals:

A_____   B_____   C_____   D_____

Scoring

Copy your totals into the appropriate boxes below. Your *highest* score is your primary style; your *second highest* score is your secondary style. If you have a tie for first place, both are primary styles.

A Score: _____ **Focuser**	**B** Score: _____ **Relater**
C Score: _____ **Integrator**	**D** Score: _____ **Operator**

MY *PRIMARY* STYLE IS: _____

MY *SECONDARY* STYLE IS: _____

Suggested Reading

▼

Alessandra, Tony. *Mastering Your Message* (audiotape). Mission, KS: SkillPath Publications, 1997.

Covey, Stephen R., *The Seven Habits of Highly Effective People: Restoring the Character Ethic*. New York: Simon & Schuster, 1989.

Fisher, Roger, and William Ury, *Getting to Yes: Negotiating Agreement Without Giving In*. New York: Penguin Books, 1981.

Jackson, Ruth Ora. "Using the PPS as an Adjunct or Alternative Instrument," *Learning 2001.* 1991, pp. 22–23.

Janda, Louis. *The Psychologist's Book of Self-Tests.* New York: Perigee, 1996.

Jung, Carl C. *Psychological Types.* New York: Harcourt & Brace, 1923.

Keirsey, David. *Please Understand Me: Character & Temperament Types,* 5th ed. Del Mar, CA: Gnosology Books, 1984.

Kroeger, Otto. *Type Talk.* Delacorte Press: New York, 1988.

O'Connor, Michael J., and Sandra J. Merwin. *The Mysteries of Motivation: Why People Do The Things They Do.* Carlson Learning Company, 1988.

Oldham, John M. *Personality Self-Portrait: Why You Think, Work, Love, and Act the Way You Do.* New York: Bantam, 1990.

Temme, Jim. *Team Power: How to Build and Grow Successful Teams.* Mission, KS: SkillPath Publications, 1996.

Available from SkillPath Publications

Self-Study Sourcebooks

Climbing the Corporate Ladder: What You Need to Know and Do to Be a Promotable Person *by Barbara Pachter and Marjorie Brody*

Coping With Supervisory Nightmares: 12 Common Nightmares of Leadership and What You Can Do About Them *by Michael and Deborah Singer Dobson*

Defeating Procrastination: 52 Fail-Safe Tips for Keeping Time on Your Side *by Marlene Caroselli, Ed.D.*

Discovering Your Purpose *by Ivy Haley*

Going for the Gold: Winning the Gold Medal for Financial Independence *by Lesley D. Bissett, CFP*

Having Something to Say When You Have to Say Something: The Art of Organizing Your Presentation *by Randy Horn*

Info-Flood: How to Swim in a Sea of Information Without Going Under *by Marlene Caroselli, Ed.D.*

The Innovative Secretary *by Marlene Caroselli, Ed.D.*

Letters & Memos: Just Like That! *by Dave Davies*

Mastering the Art of Communication: Your Keys to Developing a More Effective Personal Style *by Michelle Fairfield Poley*

Organized for Success! 95 Tips for Taking Control of Your Time, Your Space, and Your Life *by Nanci McGraw*

A Passion to Lead! How to Develop Your Natural Leadership Ability *by Michael Plumstead*

P.E.R.S.U.A.D.E.: Communication Strategies That Move People to Action *by Marlene Caroselli, Ed.D.*

Productivity Power: 250 Great Ideas for Being More Productive *by Jim Temme*

Promoting Yourself: 50 Ways to Increase Your Prestige, Power, and Paycheck *by Marlene Caroselli, Ed.D.*

Proof Positive: How to Find Errors Before They Embarrass You *by Karen L. Anderson*

Risk-Taking: 50 Ways to Turn Risks Into Rewards *by Marlene Caroselli, Ed.D. and David Harris*

Speak Up and Stand Out: How to Make Effective Presentations *by Nanci McGraw*

Stress Control: How You Can Find Relief From Life's Daily Stress *by Steve Bell*

The Technical Writer's Guide *by Robert McGraw*

Total Quality Customer Service: How to Make It Your Way of Life *by Jim Temme*

Write It Right! A Guide for Clear and Correct Writing *by Richard Andersen and Helene Hinis*

Your Total Communication Image *by Janet Signe Olson, Ph.D.*

Handbooks

The ABC's of Empowered Teams: Building Blocks for Success *by Mark Towers*

Assert Yourself! Developing Power-Packed Communication Skills to Make Your Points Clearly, Confidently, and Persuasively *by Lisa Contini*

Breaking the Ice: How to Improve Your On-the-Spot Communication Skills
by Deborah Shouse

The Care and Keeping of Customers: A Treasury of Facts, Tips, and Proven Techniques for Keeping Your Customers Coming BACK! *by Roy Lantz*

Challenging Change: Five Steps for Dealing With Change *by Holly DeForest and Mary Steinberg*

Dynamic Delegation: A Manager's Guide for Active Empowerment *by Mark Towers*

Every Woman's Guide to Career Success *by Denise M. Dudley*

Exploring Personality Styles: A Guide for Better Understanding Yourself and Your Colleagues *by Michael Dobson*

Grammar? No Problem! *by Dave Davies*

Great Openings and Closings: 28 Ways to Launch and Land Your Presentations With Punch, Power, and Pizazz *by Mari Pat Varga*

Hiring and Firing: What Every Manager Needs to Know *by Marlene Caroselli, Ed.D. with Laura Wyeth, Ms.Ed.*

How to Be a More Effective Group Communicator: Finding Your Role and Boosting Your Confidence in Group Situations *by Deborah Shouse*

How to Deal With Difficult People *by Paul Friedman*

Learning to Laugh at Work: The Power of Humor in the Workplace *by Robert McGraw*

Making Your Mark: How to Develop a Personal Marketing Plan for Becoming More Visible and More Appreciated at Work *by Deborah Shouse*

Meetings That Work *by Marlene Caroselli, Ed.D.*

The Mentoring Advantage: How to Help Your Career Soar to New Heights
by Pam Grout

Minding Your Business Manners: Etiquette Tips for Presenting Yourself Professionally in Every Business Situation *by Marjorie Brody and Barbara Pachter*

Misspeller's Guide *by Joel and Ruth Schroeder*

Motivation in the Workplace: How to Motivate Workers to Peak Performance and Productivity *by Barbara Fielder*

NameTags Plus: Games You Can Play When People Don't Know What to Say
by Deborah Shouse

Networking: How to Creatively Tap Your People Resources *by Colleen Clarke*

New & Improved! 25 Ways to Be More Creative and More Effective *by Pam Grout*

Power Write! A Practical Guide to Words That Work *by Helene Hinis*

The Power of Positivity: Eighty ways to energize your life *by Joel and Ruth Schroeder*

Putting Anger to Work For You *by Ruth and Joel Schroeder*

Reinventing Your Self: 28 Strategies for Coping With Change *by Mark Towers*

Saying "No" to Negativity: How to Manage Negativity in Yourself, Your Boss, and Your Co-Workers *by Zoie Kaye*

The Supervisor's Guide: The Everyday Guide to Coordinating People and Tasks
by Jerry Brown and Denise Dudley, Ph.D.

Taking Charge: A Personal Guide to Managing Projects and Priorities *by Michal E. Feder*

Treasure Hunt: 10 Stepping Stones to a New and More Confident You! *by Pam Grout*

A Winning Attitude: How to Develop Your Most Important Asset!
by Michelle Fairfield Poley

For more information, call 1-800-873-7545.

Notes

Notes